SUKHAMANI SAHIB:

FOUNTAIN OF ETERNAL JOY

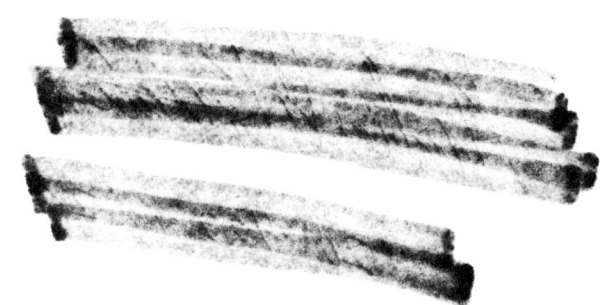

SUKHAMANI SAHIB:

FOUNTAIN OF ETERNAL JOY

Translation by
SWAMI RAMA

Introduction by K. S. Duggal

The Himalayan International Institute
of Yoga Science and Philosophy of the U.S.A.
Honesdale, Pennsylvania

©1988 by Swami Rama

Himalayan International Institute
of Yoga Science and Philosophy of the U.S.A.
RR 1, Box 400
Honesdale, Pennsylvania 18431

First Printing 1988

All rights reserved. Reproduction of this book in any manner, in whole or in part, in English or in any other language, is prohibited.

The paper used in this publication meets the minimum requirements of American National Standard for Information Sciences—Permanence of Paper for Printed Library Materials. ANSI Z39.48-1984. ∞

ISBN 0-89389-110-X

PRINTED IN THE UNITED STATES OF AMERICA

Contents

Acknowledgments	vi
Dedication	vii
Introduction by K. S. Duggal	1
Petals of Gratitude by Swami Rama	3
Canto I	7
Canto II	17
Canto III	27
Canto IV	37
Canto V	47
Canto VI	57
Canto VII	67
Canto VIII	77
Canto IX	87
Canto X	97
Canto XI	107
Canto XII	117
Canto XIII	127
Canto XIV	137
Canto XV	147
Canto XVI	157
Canto XVII	167
Canto XVIII	177
Canto XIX	187
Canto XX	197
Canto XXI	207
Canto XXII	217
Canto XXIII	227
Canto XXIV	237
About Swami Rama	246

Acknowledgments

I wish to thank Mahimah Hoffman and David Presser, who both worked very hard with me on the manuscript. Without their help, it would not have been possible to complete this task in such a short time. Dr. Shanta went through the manuscript before publication. Devika Nichols assisted in the word processing of the manuscript. Darlene Clark completed the typesetting of the text. Gopala Deva printed the book and the cover was designed by Vicki Roser. I also wish to acknowledge the inspiration of those who have previously translated and interpreted *Sukhamani Sahib*.

*Dedicated to the Guru Nanak Foundation
of New Delhi, India*

All proceeds from the publication of this book are dedicated to the Guru Nanak Foundation for the support of their work.

Introduction

Sukhamani Sahib: Fountain of Eternal Joy has also been called the Psalm or Prayer of Peace. It is a beautiful and inspiring hymn composed by Sri Guru Arjan Dev, the fifth Sikh guru. Guru Arjan Dev lived from 1563-1606. He was himself the compiler of the *Holy Granth Sahib*, the Bible of the Sikhs, and the poem/hymn called *Sukhamani* forms one part of the *Granth Sahib*. The Sikh Gurus following Guru Nanak used "Nanak" as their *nom de plume*, since it is believed that Guru Nanak reincarnated himself in the gurus who came after him.

The hymn *Sukhamani* is composed of twenty-four cantos, each of which is followed by eight stanzas. The poem is traditionally recited early in the morning by all devout Sikhs, and inspires and elevates the heart. It is a lofty and soaring statement of the beauty of the Divine in all things, and as such, soothes the mind and provides solace for those who feel themselves tossed by the storms and winds of life.

And yet, this beautiful and inspiring poem was written by a man who was no stranger to pain and life's suffering. He lived in the world, married and raised a family, and was active as a leader to his people during a time of great opposition and strife. He saw the suffering of his people and lived without indulgence or wealth. He also initiated projects to end their suffering. His notion of peace was not one of escapism from the issues of life, nor was it one of sloth or weakness—he fought injustice and was ultimately martyred for his purpose. His affirmation of joy and peace in life inspires the reader.

It is the practice of remembering the Name of the Divine that brings this peace, tranquility, and contentment to the seeker and aspirant. It is establishing oneself firmly in the practice of the Name that has the power to transform the human personality and character. This is a universal Truth of all the great teachings, which is expressed beautifully by Guru Arjan Dev in *Sukhamani Sahib*. Inner joy and contentment are the basis for all external unity and peace in life. The human being yearns always and ever for this transforming joy and sense of oneness. We live in a world which often seems to focus on conflict and differences between human beings, communities or nations. Let *Sukhamani Sahib* remind us of that level at which all human experience is One and all discord ceases. When each human being realizes and experiences this purity and union within his own mind and heart then, in truth, will we "love all and exclude none."

K. S. Duggal
New Delhi

Petals of Gratitude

If, from this pen while rhyming this verse
My thoughts and words within you disperse
Forgive and accept this, I bid you adieu.
O Nanak, great one, I revere and love you.

A guide to millions and symbol of immortality,
You lead us from profane to highest Reality.
You shed light on us from your eternal summit
Equally upon the path of householder and hermit.
Why have you forsaken your children today
When there is dire need of following your way?

These verses of *Sukhamani* are rhymed as I felt —
The way I was inspired, with humility I knelt.
Give me the strength to continue to rhyme,
Sing the name of the Lord, and your sayings sublime.

Have I ever eaten without remembering you?
Have I ever slept without praying to you, too?
Have I done my duty with my utmost care?
Darling, dearer than my soul, rarest of rare.

Grant to me a few more years to complete thy task
Then just take away this weary, mortal mask.
I became his envoy to the modern civilization
To share the message of the seers and Self-Realization.

This message for the common man, for each and
    everyone,
Includes all faiths and lands and creeds, moreover
    excludes none.
Repeatedly I prostrate to the Self-Existent One,
Remembering you in every breath with pride and vain
    undone.
Solace I find alone, inside, within my inner chamber
By murmuring your name Divine in every breath,
    remember.

Sukhamani is the fountainhead of this Divine bliss
And one who heartily recites will certainly find this.
So let you sing and swing and dance in joyous Divine
    rhythm
Or jump in joy unmeasured and the unfathomable you'll
    fathom.
Do your daily actions with a skillfully motivation,
Thus, Lord's favorite be, and serve without cessation.

I offer my undying gratitude to thee,
When lost in witchery of words, Baba, care for me.
I am no poet laureate of great public repute.
I am no epic writer of the cheering multitude.

All that I have or think or feel, to thee I do surrender;
I sing thy name in every breath, at all times I remember.
Alas, our voyage here is from the realm of the unknown —
A stay too brief upon this plane, though held within the known.
The temporal and known we see is always, ever, changing,
Alike the face of the high moon; with waxing and with waning.

We laugh and cry, we give and take, we love and then we groan.
But when the parting time has come, we walk away alone.
O Friends, then let you now recite, the blessed *Sukhamani*!
Enjoy in it the nectar of the purest Divine honey!

One thing alone, O Blessed one, I have to ask of thee —
When I depart this mortal plane, please do not forget me.

I seek no woman, friend, or fame;
I find salvation in thy name.
Thy kind and loving care I need;
Thy blissful grace alone I heed.

Renounced in youth the home where I was born;
Renunciation gifted me one morn.
I am not Brahmin, Hindu, Jew or Muslim,
And neither Sikh nor Parsi, Jain or Christian.
Belonging to the Lord of Life, alone,
Let no one else acclaim me as their own.
I follow on the path of ancient sages
As Nanak did in other times and ages.

And lastly Arjan Dev I will salute
Who wrote this joyful hymn of Absolute
And shared it with a world of strife and woe.
Thus bringing Divine joy to all who know
The secret of remembrance of the Name
That brings us joy and peace, to all the same.

Swami Rama

CANTO I

Prologue

I bow to the supreme Guru, the one divine Creator,
Who existed before time began its task
    as life's regulator;
Who reigns even still and oversees
    the world's creation;
Who eternally shall guide the world's illumination.

1

With reverence I reflect upon my Lord,
And my soul is freed from all discord;
Afflictions of mind and body cease;
My being is filled with the splendor of peace.
I reflect upon Him Whose presence sustains all,
Whose name myriad beings repeatedly recall.
The *Vedas, Puranas,* and *Smritis* affirm
That His name is the highest and holiest term;
That His name is sacred, powerful and pure;
That His name is the source of all life they assure.
If God's blessed name finds a place in one's heart —
Even a slight impression, a humble start —
Such a man finds he will receive
Praises so glorious that few can conceive.
There are those whose yearning for God is resolute,
Who live for a glimpse of the One beyond dispute.
Their influence is divine and can aid all mankind;
Bless me with the presence of God-seekers to find.

Nanak says:
Help me to remember You, Lord, in my every motion;
Free me from the waves of life's turbulent ocean.
God's name is nectar which upon men can bestow
Peace, happiness, and salvation's true glow.
God's name finds its throne in the hearts of those men
Who are saintly and devoted, pray think you of them.

2

He who remembers the name of the Lord —
The cycles of births he'll not be drawn toward.
From the anguish of dying he'll be fully exempt;
This man, the god of death can never tempt.
From the laws of mortality he will be free,
And all his enemies will surely flee.
Neither harm nor obstruction shall come his way,
For he remains conscious of God night and day.
Pain affects not the one who meditates:
For him fear has no power to intimidate.
The gift of God, to remember His name,
To meditate sincerely and His grace obtain;
This gift is learnt in the presence of those
Who, true and devoted, in God find repose.

Nanak says:
The man who for God has true love and devotion,
Will obtain treasures as vast as the ocean.

3

Remembering God, men attain the nine treasures;
Their earthly powers exceed human measures.
In this blessed pursuit divine knowledge is gained,
The secrets of wisdom and truth are explained.
Meditating, the aspirant becomes steady;
His mind focused, illumined and ready.
Remembering God, the benefits are gained
Of all rituals and austerities which may be sustained.
By continued awareness of God's presence most true,
The notion of duality shows itself undue.
Meditating, men bathe in their hearts
At the holiest shrine where His love God imparts.
The devoted are honored in the court of the Lord;
Their actions become righteous, with God in accord.
Remembering God, man surrenders his will;
With the guidance of God he can do no ill.
His life becomes fruitful, his efforts rewarded;
By God's decree all his progress afforded.
God selects those who'll follow His way.
Their efforts He guides, all is by His say.

Nanak says:
Bow at the feet of God's devotees most true,
Honor and learn from His blessed retinue.

4

The highest of duties is to remember God's name,
Many souls were uplifted while pursuing this aim.
Praising God's name, mind's restlessness is abated;
Great clarity gained, all truths elucidated;
Death loses its power to frighten the mind;
Fulfilled are men's wishes of every kind;
Mind is cleansed of filth and sin,
And filled with the nectar of God's name therein.
God dwells on the tongue of those saintly few
Whose remembrance of Him guides all things they do.

Nanak says:
There is one task my heart does crave:
Of such a saint to be a slave.

5

Those who remember God enjoy true wealth.
They alone are granted honor and spiritual health.
In the sight of the Lord
    finding acceptance and recognition,
Among men they hold a most revered position.
Remembering God's name relieves men of all need:
Independent, free of want, true kings they are indeed;
Living their lives in eternal happiness;
Freed from death and rebirth,
    they know everlasting bliss.
But only those few who the Lord does bless
Are drawn to remember Him with earnestness.

Nanak says:
Pray for the dust from the feet of those saints
Who remember God always and have no complaints.

6

Those men of God who dwell in His name
Do not seek for wealth or fame;
They lead their lives for the good of others.
I bow in reverence to these holy brothers.
Their faces radiate love and light,
Their lives are filled with peace and delight.
Remembering God, they master the mind
And lead righteous lives, leaving pettiness behind.
By dedication to the one Lord most true,
They find endless joy in all that they do.
With the help of these saints may we maintain awareness
Of God's omnipresence, and trust in His fairness.

Nanak says:
Let us wait in readiness for His grace to dawn;
Pray to be chosen, thus closer to Him drawn.

7

Remembering God, one succeeds in each endeavor;
His fears and anxieties vanish forever.
Always singing praises to God above,
His mind is transfixed by a vision of God's love.
Living in God's presence he is totally immersed.
Nothing can sway him; for God alone he has thirst.
The lotus of his heart blossoms serenely.
His ears hear the music of the heavens most keenly.
Boundless tranquility and joy men derive
From remembering God's name each moment they're alive.
Those for whom God smiles are blessed to recall
And repeat His name always, with reverence beyond all.

Nanak says:
Among these saints please grant me sanctuary,
Where I'll pray to be chosen one day His emissary.

8

The saints evolved through remembrance of God's name.
The Rishis' inspiration to write the *Vedas* was the same.
Remembrance of His name has led men to pursue
Renunciation and continence as paths of virtue.
In praise of His name men seek to give charity;
Those of humble birth become leaders with great clarity.
Upon His name the whole world does depend;
The Cause of all causes is the Lord, most reverend.
The world was created for remembering He
Who lives in His name and ever shall be.

Nanak says:
When God blesses one with understanding of this
    teaching,
The Guru's guidance brings the practice within reaching.

CANTO II

Prologue

Nanak says:
O Remover of all pain and suffering of the poor,
Who dwells in every heart now and evermore,
O God, rescuer of the helpless and the lost,
I seek your protection, You Who none can exhaust.

1

In the hereafter where there shall not be
Parents, sons, friends or brothers to befriend thee,
God's name, O my soul, your helper shall be,
A guiding Light to accompany thee.
When terrible devils of death seek to crush you,
God's name alone has power to protect you.
When insurmountable obstacles arise,
The name of God their removal will devise.
Acts of expiation shall no salvation yield;
God's name alone that power can wield.

Nanak says:
Taught by the guru, remember God, O my soul.
Myriad joys you shall obtain as you near this goal.

2

A man may be king of the world's empire,
But he'll find no peace though long he may aspire.
Only by remembering God's name in his heart,
Will the seeds of happiness take root and then start.
A man may own millions yet crave even more;
Only love of the name shuts desire's great door.
Countless mortal pleasures will not quench man's thirst;
He must drink the nectar of the name which ranks first.
Wherever a man must travel alone,
God's name shall assist him as he greets the unknown.

Nanak says:
Such a name, O my soul, cherish in your heart;
When guided by the guru, great wisdom it will impart.
Thus nurturing the name will lead you to obtain
Entry into the very highest domain.

3

Though a man possess millions of assets and friends,
It is not upon these which salvation depends.
For only by remembering God's name with devotion
Shall one manage safely to cross life's vast ocean.
When untold obstacles cause man to regress,
The name will instantly safeguard success.
One bound in the cycles of transmigration
May yet attain rest and find salvation.
So too when the soul is tarnished by conceit,
And no cleanser will cause the stain to retreat.
The name has the power to gain a man peace,
Wash sins away and man's soul release.

Nanak says:
O mind, let His name in the heart be ingrained;
In the company of saints it can be obtained.

4

In this world and beyond where the way is long,
God's name shall provide and keep you strong.
Amidst prevailing darkness and wearisome gray,
The name of God shall brighten your way.
You must travel alone, without family or friend;
But the name of God shall protect to the end.
Though you meet with constant and oppressive heat,
The name will provide a shady retreat.

Nanak says:
And when you're afflicted with insatiable thirst,
The name will rain down a nectar-filled cloudburst.

5

For a sage the name plays an essential part,
Remembered in his mind and dwelling in his heart.
For those who serve Him, God's name gives protection,
Having saved millions from harm and dejection.
With constant awareness saints praise God night and day;
His name for them all pains can allay.
God's name is a holy man's cherished treasure;
A gift from heaven of worth beyond measure.

Nanak says:
For those who love God with body, soul and mind,
God grants wisdom and knowledge of the highest kind.

6

For God's servants the name leads to salvation,
Fulfilling all needs and engendering elation.
It brings to His followers true love and beauty,
And removes all obstacles interfering with duty.
True saints feel exalted repeating His name,
And devotion to God brings them honor and fame.
Through the name they begin to truly enjoy,
As techniques of meditation they learn to employ.
From God true saints feel no separation;
In their hearts He is worshipped with full concentration.

Nanak says:
Their minds are absorbed in His name most holy.
True saints place their trust in one God solely.

7

For His servant, God's name is true wealth, a great treasure
A gift to him by God's grace and pleasure.
For him the name is a stronghold indeed
Which no worldly power can hope to succeed.
Imbued with God's love, his mind is enraptured;
The melody of God's name his heart has captured.
His mind accesses that state of meditation
Where no worldly thought can disturb concentration.
The mind of a saint dwells on God day and night;
The world can't help but be blessed by His light.

Nanak says:
Many gain salvation who love God with devotion.
In the company of saints many others cross life's ocean.

8

God's name is a heaven-grown miraculous tree
Which fulfills man's needs and helps set him free.
Songs of God possess powers of the Kamdhen cow
To fulfill men's desires here and now.
Among all sermons praise of God ranks most high;
Upon singing His praises pain and sorrow must die.
For saints the name's glory resounds in the heart,
Transforming their natures so all sins depart.
Through good fortune the company of true saints is found;
Serving them brings knowledge of the name most renowned.
In this world there is nothing to equal the name,
Yet how few the possession of this gift can proclaim.

Nanak says:
By following instructions of the guru who is true,
The name is obtained by a fortunate few.

CANTO III

Prologue

I've studied many *Shastras* and *Smritis* too;
None compare with God's name, that is true.

Nanak says:
Beyond price the nature of Its soothing grace,
No text or teaching Its wealth can embrace.

1

Recitations of texts, religious discourses;
Meditations on multiple godlike forces;
Practice of penance and long expositions
Of *Shastras* and *Smritis* on human conditions;
Practice of Yoga and religious ritual;
Renunciation of all for wandering habitual;
Efforts made to acquire merit;
Distribution of wealth and desire to share it;
Offering sacrifice and bodily mutilation;
Burning body parts as a form of privation;
Repeated fasting and taking of vows;
Testing the limits our body allows:
None of these measures equals worship of the name!
One repetition merits more than all above acts can claim.

Nanak says:
With the guru's direction, this word is more profound
Than all austerities and rituals that in the world abound.

2

A man may wander across the wide earth,
Or live a long time from the day of his birth,
Or retire from the world a religious recluse,
Or be an ascetic practicing physical abuse.
A man may sacrifice himself in the fire,
Or donate his gold and all worldly attire,
Or perform inner washes and yoga positions,
Or attempt Jain practices and their mortifying
    conditions.
He may torture his body and cut it to pieces,
But still his pride neither lessens nor ceases.
Such efforts for advancement as these cannot claim
To possess value equal to God's name.

Nanak says:
When the name is practiced as the gurus say,
It leads one along salvation's pathway.

3

A man may leave his body at a place of holiness;
However, in so doing his pride will not be less.
A man may cleanse himself religiously each day,
But the filth of the mind can't be removed this way.
One may subject his body to severe austerities,
Yet within his mind there will persist vulgarities.
The body may be washed so as to make it clean,
Yet how can this mud wall maintain real hygiene?

Nanak says:
O my soul, the glory of God's name is most great;
It has saved the lowest sinners from terrible fate.

4

Intellect can cause an increased fear of death,
Such efforts cannot quench man's thirst for life and
    breath.
Donning religious garb can't hope to cure
Man's mind of worldly thoughts and make it pure.
Countless methods a man may try;
Still for God's court he'll not qualify.
To the sky he may rise or to nether worlds go,
But the nets of the world he'll still not o'erthrow.
All attempts for liberation except for the name
Result in punishment under death's claim.
The king of death is a being most odd:
The one thing he fears is the name of God.
Repeating God's name with sincere devotion
Dissolves all pains in love's vast ocean.

Nanak says:
Effortlessly and without illusion
Remember His name in blissful profusion.

5

To attain the four boons a man must apply
Himself in the service of saints most high.
The four boons are faith, fulfillment of desires,
Wealth, and salvation for which man aspires.
If he wishes a life free of trouble and pain,
In his heart he should ne'er let praise of God wane.
A man seeking honor like his saintly brothers
Must surrender his pride for the sake of others.
A man beset with fear of transmigration
Should seek refuge with saints to ease his agitation.

Nanak says:
He who thirsts for God is blessed indeed;
A sacrifice is Nanak for him who would be freed.

6

A prince is the man who effaces his pride;
In the company of saints he chooses to reside.
One who deems himself lowly, exalted shall be;
And honored for his humble sincerity.
He whose mind is humble as the dust of all men's feet,
Will see God's presence in all men he does meet.
He whose heart is freed of evil and sin
Shall regard every man as his friend and kin.
Such men of God shall view as the same
All events in their lives, despite pleasure and pain.

Nanak says:
By good or evil they remain unaffected;
Purity of heart in their actions is reflected.

7

O God, Your name is wealth for the poor;
Shelter for the homeless, their spirits it will restore.
Honoring the lowly, their souls it uplifts;
O God, upon all You shower Your gifts.
You're the power which prompts and guides each man's action;
All hearts' secrets You know to Your satisfaction.
O God, the extent of Your glory and power
A man can't know, though long he may scour
The books and discourses available to him:
The limits of his mind make his vision too dim.
Your love of You alone is born and inspired,
By You alone can Your praises be sung and admired.

Nanak says:
The glory of Your greatness no man can discern;
You alone have the knowledge for which all men yearn.

8

The best of all religions in any society
Is remembrance of the name with faith and piety.
Of all religious rites a man can perform,
The best is to remove sin, thus himself transform.
In the company of saints this he can achieve —
Dispel all evil tendencies, then God's grace receive.
The best of all practices is for a man to hear
Repeated in his heart the name of God so dear.
Of all divine speeches the most holy to say and hear
Is the praise of Him, Who's most pure and sincere.

Nanak says:
Of all holy places most sacred is the heart,
Wherein the name of God lives and will never depart.

CANTO IV

Prologue

O man, you are of little worth,
And filled with ignorance starting from birth.

Nanak says:
O man, remember the name of the Lord;
With Him let your thoughts be ever in accord.
Dwell on God your Creator, deep in your heart;
Know that from your side He'll never depart.

1

O man, may you marvel upon the wonders of God's grace;
And recall from what origins He brought you to this place.
How he made, fashioned and adorned you, you should know
And put you safe in the fire of the womb to grow.
Remember as a babe He gave you milk to drink;
In your youth food and comforts, and power to think.
When you aged He gave many a friend
To help and serve and your needs attend.
Worthless is the man who can't appreciate
All Your favors and the goodness You radiate.

Nanak says:
O God, show mercy upon man so he may see
And come to understand the wonders of Thee.

2

O man, forget not God by Whose grace you have life;
And enjoy the Earth's comforts with family, friend and wife.
You are blessed with clean water which is cool and has flavor;
And served by precious fire and soft winds which you savor.
You enjoy many pleasures by His grace,
And are provided necessities for needs you face.
He has blessed you with hands and feet, ears, eyes and tongue;
And yet by you His praises are unsung.
Why have you abandoned God, Who blesses you each day,
And attached yourself to others in such a foolish way?
Alas, men are foolish, sinful and blind.
When immersed in ignorance, no Truth can they find.

Nanak says:
O God, save men from their pride and ingratitude;
By Your grace, restore to them a righteous attitude.

3

God, Who protects man from the time of his birth,
Is not even loved by this fool of small worth.
By serving God a man attains the nine treasures;
But foolish man seeks not God, just his own petty
    pleasures.
God is always and ever there before man's eyes;
Yet man in his blindness thinks He's above the skies.
By serving God, man could gain honor in the highest
    court;
But foolish man forgets God, his memory falls short.

Nanak says:
Alas, mortal man shall always be remiss;
Yet God the Infinite preserves all despite this!

4

Forsaking the jewel of the name, man instead
Adores a mere shell and so to maya is wed.
The Truth he dismisses; thus in its place
He brags about falsehoods which lead to disgrace.
That which is fleeting man thinks will e'er stay;
While death hovers near, man denies it away.
Attaching himself to things he must leave,
Declining the ever-present Lord to receive.
Careful to wipe any dirt from his feet,
Like a donkey he'll roll in ashes of deceit.

Nanak says:
He has fallen into a deep well of blindness.
O Lord, liberate him through your mercy and kindness.

5

The sinner is a member of the human race,
But the manners of a beast he does embrace.
Deceiving other people days and nights
With lies and insincerity, the Truth he boldly slights.
Wearing religious garb and outwardly seeming pious,
Inside his heart reveals a worldly bias.
Though trying to conceal his base personality,
No efforts can hide his lust for carnality.
He professes to be learned and practices meditation;
Performs ritual washes and lives in contemplation.
But deep within his heart the truth is always known:
He's greedy as a dog, a fact he soon must own.
Attempting to conceal passion's fire in his heart,
He applies ashes to the body and plays a saint's part.
Tied to his neck, such a weighty load of sin;
Can his hope of swimming life's ocean be but slim?

Nanak says:
Yet were the Lord to come into his life —
Such a man, absorbed in God, would quit his sin and
    strife.

6

How can a sinner, blind though he be,
Find his way by just hearing and thus be set free?
Take his hand, O God, show him the way,
So he'll reach the goal for which all men pray.
How can a deaf man understand a riddle?
Speak of night, he'll think of dawn or day's middle.
How can a man who is dumb ever sing?
His voice will first crack before sound will ring.
How can a cripple roam the mountainside?
He can't even get there, much less take a stride.

Nanak says:
To that Ocean of mercy helpless man should appeal —
For only by God's kindness can progress be real.

7

Man thinks not of the Friend ever near,
Instead loves the enemy he should fear.
In a house of sand his life is spent,
Enjoying worldly pleasures and trying to be content.
Deceived by illusion man fails to see
That his pleasures will end and so will he!
With revenge, enmity, lust and passion
He lives his life in a lowly fashion.
Such falsehood, viciousness, sin and greed —
How can deceitful man ever succeed?

Nanak says:
From life to life these deeds he does repeat.
O Lord, help man rise above his defeat.

8

O Lord, You are the Master to Whom I pray;
You are the Owner of my body and Creator of each day;
Father and Mother to men are Thee;
Children blessed by Your grace are we.
Your limits, O Lord, none can access;
You're the Highest of the high—unequalled, fathomless;
All creation is strung by Your hand;
All obey Your will and follow Your command.

Nanak says:
Your limits, O Lord, only You can see.
Always and ever I am sacrifice to Thee.

CANTO V

Prologue

Those who abandon God for worldly pleasures,
Are doomed to fail according to God's measures.

Nanak says:
A man has no honor without God's name;
In God's court he shall have no claim.

1

Receiving ten gifts from God, man shows no gratitude;
He's quick to adopt a negative attitude.
All these gifts the Lord bestows!
Let one be withheld, man's faith soon goes.
Responding with anger, in God losing trust,
For loss of one thing man feels God unjust.
If God withdrew all gifts that He gave,
What could man do? — the poor foolish knave!
Before God, man's force is of no avail;
One should bow to Him Who will prevail.
He for whom God is considered most dear
Knows joy in his heart, his way will be clear.

Nanak says:
Whosoever is blessed to accept divine will,
All needs and desires the Lord shall fulfill.

2

God is the Banker with capital to lend;
To man He entrusts it to use and to tend.
Man uses God's gifts for food and drinks,
And enjoys his life as best he thinks.
If God takes back something He'd extended,
Man becomes angry and feels offended.
Thus man loses all honor with the Lord;
To this poor fool, His trust never more will afford.
If man would relinquish the gift to its Owner,
And willingly comply with intentions of the Donor,

Nanak says:
God will shower him with blessings fourfold.
O His kindness and mercy are a wonder to behold!

3

Varied are man's attachments to worldly things,
Varied the pleasures to which he clings.
Yet one day these attachments he must release:
Worldly things pass away; and man's life, too, must cease.
Man enjoys comfort in the shadow of a tree;
When the shadow disappears he mourns the loss, regretfully.
All the eye can see is temporary;
Still blind men grip tightly to that which must flee.
Whoever gives love to one passing by
Gains nothing — the traveler will fly.
O my soul, only love of the name will bring peace,
And from maya's deception secure your release!

Nanak says:
By God this love is given to those men,
Who in His mercy He blesses again and again.

4

Perishable is man, his family and wealth;
Perishable his worldly love, ego and mental health;
Perishable is man's empire, his property and young age;
Perishable is his lust and his violent rage.
Perishable are his chariots, elephants and horses;
Perishable his attachment to pleasures and resources;
Perishable is deceit, passion and pride;
Perishable is man's arrogance, that too will subside.
All is perishable except one thing
Worship of God's name with the guru's guiding.

Nanak says:
Only through meditation on the Lord's holy feet,
Can a man live a life that is true and complete.

5

Vain are hands which steal from their brothers;
And ears which hear the slander of others;
Vain are eyes, gazing at another woman's beauty;
And the tongue, eating while forgetting God and duty.
Vain are feet which strive to do wrong;
And minds coveting things that to others belong;
Vain is the body which does not serve mankind;
And the nose which to evil smells is inclined.
Without understanding God and the name
Man's life is worthless, lacking true aim.

Nanak says:
He in whose body God's name does resound,
Finds his life fruitful, worthy and profound.

6

Pointless is man's life if he
Cannot recognize God's sovereignty.
For how can man ever hope to be pure,
When with God and the Truth he is not secure?
Useless the man who is spiritually blind;
His breath and words aren't inspired or refined.
Unless he remembers God each day,
Man's life will simply waste away;
His days and nights will pass in vain,
Like crops will ruin without the rain.
Unless inspired by God, actions have no merit,
As miser's wealth is useless because none share it.
God's embracers are blessed indeed:
Their hearts are fulfilled, they are never in need.

Nanak says:
To those saintly few who worship His name,
I offer as sacrifice myself for their aim.

7

Professing one thing and doing another,
Man attaches himself to friend and brother.
No love for God in his heart can be found;
To worldly pleasures his mind remains bound.
God the Omniscient, the Ever-Wise,
Isn't fooled by man's outer disguise.
Into the hearts of all men He can see;
With ease He can judge their sincerity.
He who won't practice that which he preaches,
Repeats lessons transmigration teaches.
Yet some men's love for God is so deep,
In their hearts His remembrance they steadfastly keep.
By the sermons of these men the world will be saved,
For the love of God in each word is engraved.

Nanak says:
Only those who please Him shall achieve
    God-realization.
At the feet of such men let us seek liberation.

8

I bow to You, Supreme One, Knower of all;
Who alone bestows honor upon creatures great and small,
Who alone makes judgments on the merits of men's deeds,
Meting out justice according to their needs.
To some He shows Himself to be near,
While to others far away He does appear.
Above all stratagems and wiles is He;
Into men's hearts he sees effortlessly.
God the Omniscient will bring to His side,
Those who He chooses to help and to guide.

Nanak says:
He who God blesses, His attendant shall be.
Always remember God, Who is true and free.

CANTO VI

Prologue

I have come for refuge with the guru divine,
And ask Him to grant this request of mine:

Nanak says:
O Lord, please have mercy and make me free
Of the anger, lust, and greed which now enslave me;
Help rid my mind of sinful pride;
Release my attachment to the world outside!

1

Remember the Lord by Whose kindness you eat
A variety of dishes, tender and sweet.
You by His kindness perfume your skin;
Think of God and attain salvation therein.
You by His kindness live in comfort at home;
Your heart from Him should never roam.
You by His kindness live with family in peace;
Remember and speak of Him, never to cease.

Nanak says:
Worldly pleasures by His kindness come to you.
Meditate on the One Who is worthy and true.

2

You by His grace alone wear satin and silk;
Why forsake Him for others, and be enamored of
 that ilk?
You by His kindness rest on your bed;
Always let His praises be sung in your head.
Men of the world by His kindness honor you;
Remember it's to God that all praise is due.
Your faith in God by His grace is maintained;
May His memory in your mind always be sustained.
With love and devotion utter God's name —
In His court you'll gain honor and fame.

Nanak says:
Then in glory you shall proceed
To your heavenly home where your soul will be freed.

3

By God's grace your body enjoys full health;
Love Him, sole Owner of all wealth.
By His grace your repute will be preserved;
Praising Him always, mind's harmony conserved.
By His grace man's faults will surely yield.
Submit to Him — all discord will be healed.
By His grace you've reached a high plateau;
Cry to Him in every breath or woe.

Nanak says:
By His grace have you a priceless form.
Love the Lord and never be forlorn.

4

Through Whose kindness gems adorn your frame,
Why hesitate to remember His name?
Through Whose kindness many animals help you;
Never forget the One Who alone can do.
Through Whose kindness property and wealth come,
Embrace Him; thy heart will never be undone.
Sitting or walking keep God in mind,
Architect of seers and those who are blind.

Nanak says:
Meditate upon ineffable God!
Now and hereafter, sorrow's path you needn't trod.

5

'Tis His that you give to charity,
Remember that most holy Entity.
Without his nod no duties can be done;
Remember the Lord, brighter than any sun.
Your form so beauteous from Him derives,
It is God Who Beauty personifies.
Your place in humanity surely is due
To God's desires, and how He does construe.

Nanak says:
In heaven's court your honor is upheld.
Let guru mold praises to Him Who's never killed.

6

To us come wondrous sounds and awesome sights,
From Him Who in all eternally delights.
Speech and movement are taken for granted;
They cannot be without His commandment.
When duties are done and programs completed
Man forgets God, thinking Him not needed.
But for you one day His bliss will arrive:
The final destiny, on which you'll thrive.

Nanak says:
Why attachment to others, forsaking the Lord?
Guru guides souls to Him, eternal reward.

7

While enjoying worldly achievements,
Keep Him in your heart and subdue bereavements.
What accrues of glory and fame
Comes from God; forgotten is His name.
Stratagems and purposes may be fulfilled,
If they by the Ever-Present have been willed.
Striving to obtain eternal Truth,
Love the One Who provided youth.

Nanak says:
Mighty Power! Who alone saves all;
Your name has ability to enthrall.

8

You who speak God's holy name,
It's He Who's speaking all the same!
Chanting praises of the Lord,
Honor the Composer of note and chord.
Lotus of the heart and knowledge divine
Are yours, if He shall so incline.
If it please the Lord He'll be your guest,
Assisting with understanding's quest.
It is from Him that all true wealth derives;
From man's own efforts nothing fructifies.

Nanak says:
At station wherever the Lord's appointed,
Quite powerless are we, not yet anointed.

CANTO VII

Prologue

Whether king or beggar, rich man or poor,
Open to you is salvation's door.
The key for entrance to that place:
Remember God's name and hope for His grace.

Nanak says:
Listen to stories of faithful men;
Conquerors of mind, who merged with God then.

1

Associating with saints your life is brightened;
Sins are removed and burdens lightened.
Associating with saints all pride will perish;
Divine knowledge comes that you will cherish.
Associating with saints brings God nearby;
Right actions become your heartfelt cry.
Associating with saints yields the jewel of His name;
And everything else really seems quite tame.

Nanak says:
The glory of saints cannot be described.
Their glory's like God's, who are sanctified.

2

In the company of saints God can be realized;
Life becomes full and never trivialized.
All the senses remain controlled;
The splendor of His name — behold!
With others man becomes humble, too;
His words assume enchanting hue.
Mind is centered, ever able,
Peaceful, still, and quite stable,

Nanak says:
Having gone beyond illusions.
God's mercy comes in great suffusions.

3

With holy company foe becomes friend;
One's inclinations toward good tend.
Henceforth harboring malice toward none,
From the right path you will never run.
No one is regarded as lowly or bad;
Everywhere Supreme Joy can be had.
Stayed are maladies of pride;
Ego too has finally died!

Nanak says:
How great are saints God alone can know.
Saints' understanding with Him shall grow.

4

Good men's company focuses the mind;
That joy comes which is most refined.
Beyond the senses lives His name;
The unbearable name you can now sustain.
Having reached a spiritual position,
The abode of the Lord becomes your condition.
Knowing the essence of all religions,
One sees God in all His renditions.

Nanak says:
Thus you shall find His name's great treasure.
Sacrificing myself for saints gives pleasure.

5

Mingling with sages, one's family is saved,
As are friends and acquaintances no longer depraved.
Thereby real wealth is obtained;
From it others are maintained.
The king of death pays homage that's due;
Angelic songs glorify you.
Sins that have stained will now depart;
Sing His ambrosial name in the heart.

Nanak says:
Your spiritual powers extend and abound.
The fruits of your birth will cynics confound.

6

Among the saints painful rituals will cease;
A saint's presence begets wonderful peace.
All darkness such company dispels;
Vanishing are the fears of hells.
Now and hereafter everything shall be all right;
Apart from Him never, with God you'll ever unite.
Your desires finally will be satisfied;
Permanent gains continue after you've died.

Nanak says:
The Supreme One resides in the hearts of sages.
Salvation's found in their inspiring adages.

7

In esteemed company the name of God is heard,
His praises sung with nearly every word.
There the Lord remains in your head;
Troubles flee, salvation comes instead;
Love for the Almighty is held most dear;
He appears in everyone's heart so clear.
There we learn how to surrender
To our Lord Who is so tender;

Nanak says:
All ills heal, fulfillment is complete.
Being with saints is good fortune replete.

8

Even the *Vedas* know saints' greatness partially;
Greatness described therein is merely sensory.
Yet saints' greatness supersedes what one sees,
Infinite and beyond ephemeralities.
Highest of the high is the glory of the saint,
Stupendous, magnificent, certainly most great,

Nanak says:
Immeasurable and to them alone belonging.
Little distinguishes a saint from the King.

CANTO VIII

Prologue

Signs of the ideal man are these:
He alone remembers God always,
And speaks often of Him most high;
Worshipping none but God with heart's cry,

Nanak says:
Seeing nothing but the Lord everywhere.
These signs of the saint are sure to be there.

1

Living amidst worldly impurity
The ideal man stays pure, to God a devotee,
Like a lotus unmoved by mud beneath the sea,
Sinless and pious, a blazing sun
Burning the transgressions of everyone.
He views all with equal affection,
As benevolent wind gives protection,
To rich and poor a friendly companion.
Whether praised or scorned, he remains serene;
Like the earth, unchanged, plowed or esteemed.

Nanak says:
The God-awakened being resembles fire.
His nature burns impurities in those who aspire.

2

Purest of the pure are ideal men,
Like water that contains no pollution.
Divine light illumines his mind,
As sky covers earth, blessing mankind.
Being devoid of all pride,
With friend and foe he's satisfied.
Most exalted of everyone,
He's humility's paragon.

Nanak says:
Ideal men are only those
On whom God's grace has been transposed.

3

An awakened one becomes dust at man's feet;
None other partakes of bliss so complete.
Extending loving kindness to all,
From him no evil to man will befall.
Offensive distinctions he will not make
Between men; his eyes rain nectar for all's sake.
Free from any entanglement
His life's serene, as God has meant.

Nanak says:
This man's soul drinks divine knowledge.
Meditations on God such men pledge.

4

The ideal one fixes his hopes on the Lord;
Never perishing, he escapes death's sword.
Always most humble is he,
Serving others joyfully.
Keeping free from worldly constraint,
Self-control belongs to the saint.
Only good issues from men of this kind,
Who have left purposeless actions behind.

Nanak says:
Saved are those within the orbit of a saint.
Such a man helps everyone to contemplate.

5

An ideal man's life reflects the Great One
Who is his sole and constant companion.
His family and home are God's name,
Which moreover does the sage sustain.
Ever-watchful against sin's feint,
Banishing egoism's restraint,
With supreme bliss the heart's refrain,
His life belongs to joy's domain.

Nanak says:
This man shall forever death defy.
To heaven's peaceful abode he'll fly.

6

God-realized man knows the Lord,
Who alone is the One adored.
Life's events stream spontaneous
For saints whose motives never are heinous.
It is God Who helps man become ideal;
Man's glory is then definitely real.
Fortune having bestowed a glance of such a one,
Sacrificing self to him can now be done.

Nanak says:
Gods like Shiva search for men as these.
Saints become the Holy of holies.

7

The ideal one truly is priceless;
All virtues his soul does possess.
We cannot fathom his mystery,
And must bow to the one who is free.
Words cannot be written to interpret him,
Who has now become the lord of creation.
His greatness extends beyond measurable degree;
Only such a one as he can know his soul's beauty,

Nanak says:
So limitless is his spirituality.
To bow in reverence before him is our duty.

8

A man raised so high becomes creator of the world;
Living forever, death's power he has annulled.
Conferring benefits temporal and spiritual;
Setting defects right, all perfections he will cull.
Refuge for those forsaken by hope!
The saint protects all who cannot cope.
Proprietor of this vast sphere,
One with the Formless and without peer,

Nanak says:
He's comparable to no thing.
This man's a universal king.

CANTO IX

Prologue

Nanak says:
He who never forgets God's name,
Who in all things the Lord does proclaim,
Who at all times to Him does cling,
Is the true monk called 'touch-nothing'.
One like this is hard to find,
And capable of saving mankind.

1

The tongue of such a monk would not touch lies,
Whose heart for Immaculate God cries.
The eyes would not touch other women's beauty,
Who serves the common good gleefully.
The ears would not touch slander
Who the worst about himself can aver.
Never by guru's grace would he touch illusion,
Who the battle with low desires has won,
Nor would he touch deadly passion,
Who the fleshly demands can shun.

Nanak says:
One among millions has the restraint
To be a real touch-nothing saint.

2

A monk who truly worships Vishnu
Is one who with grace God will imbue.
Such a Vaishnav' holy man,
Immune from all worldly mammon,
Performs good deeds seeking no reward;
He's a true Vaishnav', not by God ignored.
Giving up the fruits of his labor,
Only God's glory will he savor.
The Lord's name pervades the body and mind
Of him most merciful to humankind.

Nanak says:
Who remembers the name and helps others to do likewise,
Is truly a Vaishnav and acquires salvation's prize.

3

A true 'Bhakti' is one who loves God,
Having abandoned the sinner's squad.
Removing all mental duality,
He worships omnipresent Reality.
Living with saints will clean all stain,
Counsels wisdom from his brain.
He toils for the Lord the whole day through,
With body and soul every moment anew.

Nanak says:
Keeping divine instructions in his heart,
A Bhakti knows God before he must depart.

4

Controlling his mind to serve the Almighty
Is the Pandit, devoted to His name's memory.
Drinking that name he preaches
Of God, 'till all he reaches.
Remembering the Lord's wise counsel,
Not again on earth will he dwell.
Reading the *Vedas, Puranas* and *Smritis,*
He knows this world bends to unseen decrees.

Nanak says:
Who imparts the Divine to every caste,
That Pandit deserves homage so vast.

5

The seed of His name will sprout in all;
Each of the castes may His name recall.
Who repeats God's name obtains salvation;
Practicing with saints merits admiration.
If by God's grace His name resides in the heart,
Even the lowly from Him will not be apart.
That great name can cure all disease;
Singing His praise gives joy that will please.

Nanak says:
Neither religion nor reason can provide the name.
That gift is free for those who are destiny's aim.

6

In whose heart plays the Lord's ballad,
Can truly be called the servant of God.
He alone sees all-pervading Soul;
The slave of God's slaves is his role.
He for whom God is nearest of all,
Gains acceptance in His council-hall.
When the Lord grants heavenly grace,
Then one knows reality's inmost face.

Nanak says:
Whose soul amidst life's bustle remains unattached,
Truly serves God until by death he's snatched.

7

He who obeys God's will with pleasure,
Obtains salvation during his life's measure.
This 'jivan-mukti' meets joy and grief equally;
Never apart from the Lord, he's forever happy.
God and mud are to him the same,
Nectar and poison have equal claim;
Honor and disgrace of like disdain,
Prince and beggar equally germane.

Nanak says:
For a jivan-mukti, God's ways are the best.
Though here, he's attained immortality's nest.

8

Owner of all is the Being supreme;
Wherever He lives gets named in this dream.
Our power to act emanates from Him;
What pleaseth the Lord some day must happen.
Endlessly manifesting as waves of creation
Is God, His ways not subject to interpretation.
Only known by light He gives,
The Almighty ever lives.

Nanak says:
O merciful One, our sins please forgive!
Remembering Him, joy becomes your captive.

CANTO X

Prologue

Many are those who praise the Lord,
That vast Ocean without a shore.

Nanak says:
Endless are objects created by Thee;
Uncountable too their variety.

1

Countless persons worship God,
Likewise those who through duty plod.
Countless ones live at sacred places;
As many wander in tree-filled spaces.
Countless listen to Scriptures read,
And numerous austerities' paths tread.
Countless ponder in holy musing,
Or think of Him while poetry perusing.

Nanak says:
Countless invent new names for the Lord.
His greatness extends ever more and more.

2

How many the ones who are puffed with pride;
So too those in whom ignorance does reside.
How many misers with hearts of stone,
Indifferent when hearing others moan!
How many steal belongings of another;
Millions slander against their brother.
How many work years amassing great fortune;
Also those who to exotic lands run.

Nanak says:
All must follow appointed roles.
The Lord has composed destiny's scrolls.

3

Millions are monks, celibates and seers;
Likewise kings, in pleasure believers.
Vast numbers of birds and snakes have been born;
Myriads of trees and stones do earth adorn.
Trillions are winds, waters and things fiery,
And too the realms and regions earthly.
Unnumbered the suns, moons and starry things,
As are gods, demons and heavenly kings.

Nanak says:
Everything created must obey God's command.
He saves who He chooses, and none can countermand.

4

Many men are serene or lively;
Or ruled by passion, that's God's variety.
Many holy books tell one how to be:
Vedas, Puranas, Shastras and *Smritis.*
Many jewels have been formed in the ocean,
And creature were made who have locomotion.
Many are insects whose lives are short,
And larger beings of a different sort.
Many hills and golden mountains exist
With powers watching, so their wealth will persist.
Many devoted to evil, music or wealth are created,
As are sprites, ghosts and spirits, by man unappreciated.

Nanak says:
The Lord is near to all, yet wide is his range,
God pervades all but is separate, though it seems strange.

5

Myriads in nether regions dwell,
And many live in heaven and hell.
Billions are born into human bodies;
Many swept along by transmigration's breeze.
Countless are those who avoid exertion;
Many overwork earning their portion.
Millions become wealthy through fortune's grace;
Many become anxious as gold they chase.

Nanak says:
Yet God decides the positions we hold.
Everything depends on what He has foretold.

6

Only when the Lord dwells in your heart,
Can you truly play His servant's part,
And see Omniscient God, the Sight all crave;
Then you will know you're the slave of His slaves.
Always feeling the Lord close by,
A place at His court you will occupy.
Should the Lord confer His grace on you,
Divine knowledge comes: you see what is true.

Nanak says:
Who lives unattached though busy with life,
Truly serves God, avoiding fruitless strife.

7

Creation contains countless higher regions,
And lower fields full of animated legions.
There are infinite species of beings,
So many times do these happenings
Occur; different worlds each does yield.
But God is changeless, not needing to be healed.
Millions of kinds of things were created,
And return to Him where they emanated.

Nanak says:
None can know the limits of the Lord.
God is All in all, above all He's adored.

8

Many obtain God's love through service,
Thus receiving mental bliss.
Many try to know things' essence,
And see just His holy Presence.
Many drink the nectar of God's name;
Immortality they can claim.
Many who sing His name's renown
Become absorbed in peace profound.

Nanak says:
The Lord remembers and protects devotees.
Such persons assuredly God do please.

CANTO XI

Prologue

God is Cause above all causes.
Doer of all acts in which man pauses.

Nanak says:
I sacrifice myself to the One
Who pervades water, sky and every region.

1

Only the Lord has power to do;
Only what pleases Him shall come anew.
With no restriction to His power,
The universe He can quickly devour.
His will alone supports all creation
(Finally absorbed by His inhalation).
From His orders work the exalted and lowly;
Various dramas are performed by His decrees.

Nanak says:
Everywhere the Lord enjoys His greatness.
Contained in all things is the Oneness.

2

When the Lord pleases, man is saved,
And sinners no more perish in the grave.
When the Lord pleases, life can be restored
To dead bodies, who their Maker adore.
When the Lord pleases, the fallen shall rise;
God does what He wants with all He supplies.
The Lord of this world and the next
Enjoys life's dramas, performed from His text.

Nanak says:
All actions occur according to His will.
None other possesses His masterful skill.

3

What can mere mortals accomplish alone?
All is ordained by the One on the throne.
Had man the power, his desires would rule;
But God keeps that power, not being a fool.
Ignorant men are drawn toward sin;
Were men wise, salvation they could win.
Misled by delusions mind wanders about,
Returning from vain imaginings in doubt.

Nanak says:
When most merciful God gives us His love,
Man shall absorb the name of Him Who's above.

4

O Lord, so gentle to the humble!
Promotes to king those who did stumble.
One who now is so obscure,
God can make fame's paramour.
If the Lord gives a man holy grace,
The account of his deeds the Lord will erase.
Belonging to Him is soul and body;
In every heart appears the Almighty.

Nanak says:
The framework of the world comes from the One.
I live to behold the glory He's done.

5

Man's power is not in his own command;
All power to God he must remand.
Man's course should simply be to obey,
For God ultimately has His way.
Man hopes and hopes and then despairs;
He's anxious but finally forgets his cares.
At times he blames, at times he praises;
Man explores the heavens and endures depression's crazes.

Nanak says:
He may obtain the knowledge divine.
God unites with man when He feels it is time.

6

Man can be clever in various guises;
Or sleeping all day he never rises.
He appears monstrous due to rage,
Or becomes as humble as a sage.
Man fancies himself a mighty king;
The beggar's tune he can also sing.
Although he may be very esteemed,
At times his repute cannot be redeemed.

Nanak says:
Man lives as the Lord prefers, forsooth.
By the grace of the guru I speak this truth.

7

Some men are scholars giving religious discourses;
Others are silent, contemplating finer forces.
Some men bathe at sacred places;
Others preach divine knowledge in market spaces.
The soul may wander into many forms,
As those of elephants, moths or worms.
Many are the roles man assumes for the Lord,
Dancing to the hymn of the music He's scored.

Nanak says:
Whatever God wills surely comes to be.
Certainly there is none other but He.

8

A moment may occur in the life of a man
When he finds the fellowship of a holy clan,
Never returning to his old ways again.
His life has been blessed with divine light.
In this awakened state of great insight,
Man feels his course now to be right.
His body and mind are filled with the bliss
Of the name of the One Who his soul does miss;
Remaining with God is a privilege now His.

Nanak says:
Man's soul merges with the Lord's, as water blends
With water; wanderings end — eternal peace He sends.
To sacrifice for God is where my heart tends.

CANTO XII

Prologue

Nanak says:
Happy are those who are meek,
And who self-effacement seek.
But those who suffer from pride,
From them God always will hide.

1

He who feels the kingly pride,
Like a dog in hell will reside.
Who thinks himself so very handsome,
Returns as a worm who lives in scum.
The man enamored with what he's achieved,
Shall many times be born and deceased.
You who are proud of riches and property,
Are foolish and ignorant and cannot see.

Nanak says:
When the Lord places humility in your heart,
Salvation comes now; peace when you depart.

2

Rich men counting their wealth should know,
Not one coin to the next world can go.
Generals relying on men and arms
Can swiftly incur many harms.
The one who thinks he's grander than all,
In a moment is subject to death's call.
Anyone with overbearing pride,
The heavenly Judge will soon deride.

Nanak says:
Who removes his pride by guru's grace,
Shall enter God's court's holy place.

3

Performing good deeds with inflated ego
Is vain; from them no fruit comes, only woe.
One who is proud of doing penance
Will never be one of heaven's tenants.
Hard effort without a heart that's soft,
Cannot raise man to God's court aloft.
He who deems himself full of virtue
Goodness shuns, much to his rue.

Nanak says:
Having true humility before all,
Man obtains glory and fame that won't pall.

4

A man who thinks himself the doer
Never finds peace, that is sure.
Taking credit for what has been attained,
Man wanders from life to life in pain.
Mistaking the Lord as friend and enemy,
Your mind will always be full of debris.
As long as worldly joys attract one,
Suffering shall come from divine correction.

Nanak says:
Illusion's bonds break by the Lord's grace.
With the guru's kindness man can himself abase.

5

Rich men hunger after silver,
Greed ever holds them prisoner.
Indulging in varied evil pleasures,
Happiness is ruined by these gestures.
Without contentment there is no peace;
Life's dreamy illusions never cease.
Supreme joy lies in loving His name;
Destiny's favored few excel at that game.

Nanak says:
It all depends on the One with the power.
Remember the name of the holy Endower.

6

All power to do resides with God.
Man's power to act is just a facade,
And he becomes whatever the Lord will;
Apart from God there is only nil.
Things exist in accordance with His pleasure;
He is with all, yet from all He's obscure.
Understanding all, God grades life's tests;
He's One, yet in many forms manifests.

Nanak says:
Neither coming nor going, He's never born nor dies;
Within every created thing God lies.

7

The Lord's the One Who teaches,
And the student who He reaches.
The process itself derives from the King,
And takes place within His mighty Being,
Whose Presence pervades every place.
There can be no creation outside His space.
Actor and Actress in life's daily plays,
Producer and Director of all He surveys,

Nanak says:
Indweller and container of every mind.
Indescribable worth is Thine.

8

O Lord, You are ever, ever true;
So say those blessed by a guru.
Your creation's never flawed;
The few knowing this are overawed.
Thy Form is verily most excellent;
Boundless, dazzling and magnificent.
Words from You are pure music,
Removing everything mentally caustic.

Nanak says:
Your name is poetry most holy.
Remembering Your name means loving Thee.

CANTO XIII

Prologue

Nanak says:
Who has saints' protection
Acquires salvation.
Who slanders those saints
Endures rebirth's plaints.

1

Defaming good men
Hastens your end;
Peace disappears;
One suffers hell's fears.
Wisdom is shrouded,
Fame disavowed.
Rejected by the sage,
With pain none can assuage,
Wherever one paces
Has pollution's traces.

Nanak says:
If a merciful saint accepts this knave,
Only then will the fellow be saved.

2

Slandering a saint one goes awry;
His speech resembles a raven's cry.
Slandering a saint makes one return
In the body of a snake or a lowly worm.
Slandering a saint invites much greed;
Cheating everyone becomes your creed.
Slandering a saint, you lose influence;
Extreme meanness no doubt will commence.

Nanak says:
Slandering a saint, one will have no shelter.
You'll still get salvation if the saint should prefer.

3

To speak against a sage will hurt;
Rest for the speaker will ever avert.
For a cruel heartless fiend
The Lord has words that are obscene.
Prosperity flees from such a beast:
Misery enjoys a feast!
Illness too attacks this one,
Who never with God has union.

Nanak says:
Speaking against a sage is a great mistake.
Should the sage wish, he can save a man so opaque.

4

Who thinks evil of a saint is impure;
The friendless state he shall endure.
Roaming about just like a convict,
Censure on him others will inflict.
This creature is full of pride,
And commits acts men deride.
Never escaping karma's wheel,
Peace or pleasure he'll not feel.

Nanak says:
O'er the earth he'll no home find;
Unless the saint to him be kind.

5

Slanderers of saints complete nothing;
Dreaming of success, they go on hoping.
Persons like these are always confused,
Mistaking the right path, ever bemused.
Men like these are empty within,
Just like the dead who've left life's din.
Nothing in their lives gives fruit;
The seeds they plant will grow no shoot.

Nanak says:
Slanderers of saints none will protect.
Saints can such men to heaven direct.

6

Wishing saints ill, one loses one's breath,
Like a fish out of water hastens toward death.
One will never be content,
Wanting more like fire that's spent.
The slanderer becomes isolated,
Like sesame stalks whose seeds have been crated.
The man who slanders is void of what's true,
The thoughts he speaks completely askew.

Nanak says:
His nature is fixed by the Lord's decree.
Events occur according to God's recipe.

7

Who slanders a saint is a being deformed;
His errors God's court will him inform.
Who slanders a saint neither lives nor dies;
Always in between, ever tantalized,
No hope of his can be achieved.
He's in despair and stays bereaved.
Desires persist if you slander a saint;
A man becomes what his intentions create.

Nanak says:
No one avoids the trend of his deeds,
Known only to God, this one concedes.

8

All hearts are His Who causes their formations;
To Him we give our frequent oblations.
Praise the Almighty night and day,
Remembering constantly is man's way.
The Lord's choices have to occur;
What He wills becomes man's to endure.
He's the Player in His play;
Him no one can ever sway.

Nanak says:
God grants His holy name to those
Who fortune and God's grace bring close.

CANTO XIV

Prologue

Nanak says:
O good men, leave off worldly cleverness;
Remember the Lord, Remover of distress.
Make Him the focus of all your hope;
Fears and troubles no more will develop.

1

Relying on fellow man is absurd;
God alone is the Giver, rest assured!
His gifts will satisfy our wants;
We'll no more visit hunger's haunts.
God alone keeps man alive, or will kill
The man whose own power surely is nil.
Happiness comes from accepting His will;
His name in your heart shall ever fulfill.

Nanak says:
Always remember the Lord — always;
Then harm cannot invade your days.

2

O sing the Formless One's praises;
For actions this provides a sound basis.
Keep your tongue pure by the nectar of His name;
Your soul shall be happy ever again.
With your eyes behold His splendor;
When with saints, others you'll abhor.
Your feet should walk on the path of the Lord,
Whereby all sins will be ignored.

Nanak says:
With ears hear His words, with hands do His work;
Your face will shine, and you God will not shirk.

3

Those who sing praises of Him
Are blessed in a world so grim.
Those who meditate on the holy One,
Have riches and wealth which are never undone.
Those whose heart and words speak His name,
Have peace and happiness as their claim.
Those who see behind all a Unity,
Understand what now and hereafter may be.

Nanak says:
Who realizes God by remembering his Name,
Alone can His Absolute aspect explain.

4

A man who with guru's grace introspects
Knows his smallness, and no more worldly things
　　collects.
A man lauding God in saintly company
From all disease becomes quite free.
A man singing frequently of Thee, O Lord,
Loses desires though he be a family contributor.
For a man placing hopes on God alone,
Mortality's hold can be overthrown.

Nanak says:
He who yearns for God to see,
Will never feel pain's tyranny.

5

He who always has God in his heart
Lives ever in sainthood, doing his part.
He to whom God's grace appears,
How can he have any fears?
He then sees God in His true immanence,
Penetrating creation with His Presence.
Unceasingly searching for Him, one succeeds;
With the guru's help, one realizes what he needs.

Nanak says:
He's the Mind as well as the manifest world;
The Lord himself causes creation's swirl.

6

Nothing is born, nothing dies;
God is cavorting, and all does comprise.
What comes or goes, whether visible or not,
Obeys the Producer's commands for this plot.
Self-existent and pervading all,
He creates and destroys the great and the small.
The Lord is impervious to any decay;
All events happen according to His say.

Nanak says:
He's incomprehensible, unseen and glorious;
We remember His name if He permits us.

7

They who know the Lord are honored;
The world is saved by hearing their word.
These servants of God can uplift all,
Relieving the sorrow that does them befall.
God unites with His helpers who practice
The guru's word; repeating His name leads to bliss.
Servers of the true saints will acquire
Good fortune and grace, which man do inspire.

Nanak says:
Who repeats His name gains mental detachment.
These men are most pious, and need not repent.

8

The acts of God's servant are done to obey
Him by Whose side the servant will stay.
Divine will directs the events that occur;
God alone is the Doer, all servants concur.
Whatever He does pleases His servant,
Who views the Almighty from a true slant.
The servant's absorbed in the One Who gave life;
That servant is worthy of peace so rife.

Nanak says:
God honors Himself when He honors His servant;
For the Lord and His servant are one, I do grant.

CANTO XV

Prologue

God possesses all perfections;
Knows the pains of His creations.

Nanak says:
Remember Him and you'll be saved;
Everything to Him alone I gave.

1

The Lord joins all deserted ones,
And cherishes His living sons.
He looks to their needs with solicitude;
None coming from Him will have to brood.
Don't ever forget most holy God!
He's always there during life's promenade.
Man gets nothing by his own effort,
No matter how much his desire he supports.

Nanak says:
None but the Lord is of any avail;
Remember His name — you will not fail.

2

One who is handsome should be not proud;
God's light is within every human shroud.
Nor should possession of wealth make one vain;
The Lord is the true Source of all gain.
Every great hero should readily know,
God's borrowed power allows his to show.
Givers of gifts to charities
Should learn it's all His, these varieties.

Nanak says:
Who by guru's grace has tamed his ego,
Is free from disease and emits health's glow.

3

As a pillar provides strength to the roof of a home,
The guru sustains the mind, not letting it roam.
As a stone in a boat is floated across the river,
Man crosses life's ocean when to guru he defers.
As the light of the lamp will darkness rescind,
Seeing the guru one becomes illumined.
As the light saves a traveller lost in a forest,
A guru helps man find his own light; he is blest.

Nanak says:
I want the dust of such a saint's feet;
Fulfill my heart's desire—to God I entreat!

4

O foolish mind, why must thou plaint?
You have to endure destiny's constraint.
Pleasure and pain depend on your deed;
The Lord is the only One you should heed.
Whatever He sends, accept with joy;
Why wander around like a lost boy?
What did you bring when entering the womb,
Like a greedy moth who would pleasure consume?

Nanak says:
Ever remember God's name in your heart;
With honor, to your true home you will depart.

5

You came here as a merchant for the fortune of God's name;
In the marketplace of saints it can be obtained.
As purchase price give up ego and surrender your mind;
Weigh the name in your heart's scales; you'll no longer be blind.
Carrying the name, set out with saints on that most favored trip;
Abandon all entanglements which may cause you to slip.
All will shout your honor at departure from the port;
Your face will beam when you arrive at the Lord's holy court.

Nanak says:
Trading in His name are few;
I sacrifice to those who do.

6

Wash the saint's feet and drink that nectar;
Dedicate yourself to a chosen rector.
Bathe yourself in the dust of the guru;
Sacrifice life to his wider view.
Serving the guru is rare good fortune;
Sing God's praises when you're his companion.
As you sing taste immortality;
The guru will protect his devotee.

Nanak says:
Who has shelter from the guru revered,
Gets comfort and peace which are so dear.

7

God can revive the ones who are dead,
It's He Who gives the hungry their bread.
His glance scatters treasures of every kind;
What God has ordained determines what men find.
All belong to the One Omnipotent;
Only He exists in this whole extent.
O man, think of Him always and forever;
To this sacred action, at all times endeavor.

Nanak says:
When the Lord most kind gives us His Name,
Our life becomes with purity aflame.

8

To a man with full faith in his guru,
A vision of God will surely ensue.
He becomes known everywhere as a sage,
And loves the Lord more than any can gauge.
His life and acts are verily true;
Truth is in his heart and every word new.
He sees only Truth and embodies It too;
Truth is in all, and all from It grew.

Nanak says:
Who knows that God and Truth are one
Is absorbed in Him, all else he does shun.

CANTO XVI

Prologue

Nanak says:
God hasn't form nor hue or feature;
The sensory world is not His teacher.
Those with whom the Lord is well pleased
Get knowledge of Him, their hunger appeased.

1

Give up dependence on human love;
Keep your thoughts on the One above.
Beyond the Lord there is only null;
Pervading what lives is Thee most wonderful.
God sees all, comprehending everything;
He is deep, profound and very discerning.
The Almighty though possessing supremacy,
Is a fount of kindness, forgiveness and mercy.

Nanak says:
As His humble slave, I only desire
To fall at the feet of those who know the Sire.

2

The Lord fulfills desires and protects those who seek;
What comes to pass is fixed when the Lord decides to speak.
In the blink of an eye He destroys and creates;
None knows His purpose or why He contemplates.
Man finds eternal joy and happiness
And all else he wants in the Lord's palace.
He's the highest of Kings, and the Adept of all yogis;
Supreme among penitents and those with families.

Nanak says:
Saints ever remember Him and obtain bliss.
None finds the limits of this infinite Edifice.

3

God's world-play is entirely without end;
Not even angels know what it does portend.
A child cannot fathom his father's source;
On God's will men are strung like beads, perforce.
Servants with knowledge, meditation and wisdom alone
Realize the presence of His name, which they do intone.
All others are led astray by the senses;
To transmigration they must acquiesce.

Nanak says:
Visions high and visions low belong to the Lord.
God decides just how far mankind can explore.

4

God's containers are various, and diverse are His ways;
He assumes many guises within self-consistency's rays.
However much the Lord spreads out,
He's indivisible, One throughout.
His Presence is dispersed so fine,
He plays all roles while using no time.
The scenes are also arranged by the Lord,
Who extols the worth of His acting corps.

Nanak says:
It is He Who owns all hearts and places.
I am among those who His name embrace.

5

The name of God supports all creatures,
As well as the universe and its features.
The name supports nether regions and skies,
The people and the homes they occupy.
The urge for His name inspired *Smritis, Vedas* and
    Puranas;
Those who listen are saved by the name, and reach
    Nirvana.
The name supports the three worlds and fourteen spheres;
Man will be saved by attending to the name with his
    ears.

Nanak says:
When by God's mercy a man assimilates the name,
Spirituality's heights he shall surely gain.

6

God is true in form and in every place;
His personality is Truth, never effaced.
God's character, acts and words are true;
His words in all beings are imbued.
God's creation is true and likewise His deeds;
The tree produced is true, as are all God's seed.
God's commands are the purest of the refined;
Those who know this maintain a joyous mind.

Nanak says:
The true name of God provides a great sum;
The guru alone gives the faith that does come.

7

The words and instructions of the guru are true;
Who accepts his teaching will no more rue.
When the potency and value of Truth are known,
One remembers the name and reaches salvation's zone.
He sees that God is true, and so too His creation;
The Lord alone knows His range, scope, and extension.
The Maker of all does with all what He will;
Discussing creation, one seems an imbecile.

Nanak says:
The ways of God are screened from His progeny.
What pleases the Lord must some day come to be.

8

Who comprehends how great God is,
Gets lost in wonderful spiritual bliss.
Through Truth God's servants with love are suffused,
And fulfill desires by words the guru produced.
Now His servants can salve others' pain,
And help the whole world become more sane.
Fortunate is he who may serve a sage;
His love for God will be engaged.

Nanak says:
A servant sings the praises of the Lord.
With the guru's grace, he obtains reward.

CANTO XVII

Prologue
In the beginning the Lord was true,
Ages ago, when there were not two.

Nanak says:
He is still true since the world's debut;
Veracity will never the Lord eschew.

1

The words and followers of God are true;
His worship and worshippers are of like hue.
True is His vision and those who attain it;
True is His name and whoever sustains it.
True is God Himself, and all He has made;
He is Virtue, granting it though not paid.
God's words are true, as are their speakers;
Attending to Him is true, likewise praises of seekers.

Nanak says:
Who knows God exists sees the truth of creation.
God's eternal truth can be denied by no one.

2

Who keeps the Lord near his heart in truth's form,
Sees Him as the root from which all is born.
Who has the belief that God exists,
Gets knowledge divine, especially the gist.
This kind of man loses all fear;
To the Source of his being he then becomes near,
Melting completely into the One,
So that they're in perfect union.

Nanak says:
This can be known if you understand.
When the two meet, God enfolds a man.

3

The servant of God is always obedient;
Always at worship is this suppliant.
His faith in God is most secure;
His conduct and life are very pure.
Deeply feeling the Lord within,
The servant loves Him more than his kin.
The Lord will see to every need;
Protecting your honor is part of His creed.

Nanak says:
To serve the Lord is a wonderful thing.
With every breath to Him do cling.

4

Drawing a veil over the servant's faults,
God protects His servant's honor from assaults.
Conferring glory on the servant,
God gives him the name, ending his hunt.
God cherishes the servant's high repute;
None finds his limits, no matter how astute.
Equalling servants is not to be done;
They are highest of the high, a phenomenon.

Nanak says:
Those in God's service, to whom none compare,
Soon are renowned and known everywhere.

5

Millions of men can be killed by an ant
Infused with God's power, without which it can't.
If God does not wish one's life to end,
He protects the life of His human friend.
Trying to save oneself without the Lord
Comes to nothing, it must be underscored.
To kill or preserve depends on God alone;
The Lord will protect all things that are grown.

Nanak says:
Why are you so anxious, O man?
Remember the wonderful, incomprehensible Artisan.

6

Repeating the name of the Lord evermore,
Body and soul are edified by this nectar.
Obtaining the jewel of the name, a devotee
Sees no charms in anything but Thee.
God's name is his treasure, beauty, and joy;
A comfort and companion, his spirit buoy.
Those drinking deep of the nectar of Name,
Find body and soul absorbed with its flame.

Nanak says:
Remembering the name is a constant practice
Of the Lord's servants, who must not be remiss.

7

Singing God's praises day and night
Is a gift from Him, a holy rite.
Devoted to God with yearning soul,
Servants repose in Him with self controlled.
Leaving events in the hands of Him,
Servants obey their Master's whim.
The greatness of servants is beyond my word;
I admire them in measure that's quite unheard.

Nanak says:
Who lives in God's presence all through the day,
From perfection that one will never stray.

8

Get from men as these your shelter;
Soul and body to them surrender.
Once God has been found by them,
Generosity becomes their yen.
Serve the one who's reached the Lord;
Seeing him sins are no more.
Leave aside your clever schemes
And join the Lord's servants' teams.

Nanak says:
Coming and going for you shall end.
To the feet of His servant you should attend.

CANTO XVIII

Prologue

Nanak says:
The true guru is surely the one who
Knows that personal God known by few.

Singing God's praises with the guru,
Salvation becomes one's just due.

1

A guru looks after disciples' needs;
Kindness to students he always feeds.
Removing the dirt from the aspirant's mind,
He instructs that God's name is where to incline.
The guru then breaks all worldly bonds:
Recoiling from sense pleasures, a student goes beyond.
The guru provides the wealth of the Name
To his fortunate student, so he'll reach his aim.

Nanak says:
The guru creates the future and present,
Loving his disciple with love that God sent.

2

A student who remains in his teacher's school,
Obeying the guru's every rule;
Who abnegates himself every way,
Remembers God's name through night and day,
And surrenders his mind to the guru revered,
Succeeds in the purpose he holds so dear.
Serving his guru with no thought of reward,
A student unites with the beloved Lord.

Nanak says:
It is God's kindness that makes one pursue
Pure knowledge which comes from a guru.

3

A sincere disciple who passes every test
Will meet the Lord, ending his quest,
Helped by the guru who's full of God's Name.
Again and again I'd give him my frame!
The guru gives life and all other treasure;
Day and night God's love does him allure.
The guru is in God, and God in the guru;
No doubt God is One, and never two.

Nanak says:
One's own devices will fail to find
A true guru, without grace that's divine.

4

Glimpsing the guru purifies a man;
Touching his feet will all defects ban.
Living with the guru a man learns to sing
Hymns which lead to the Supreme Being.
The guru's words will satisfy and please;
The spirit gets rest and the mind surcease.
A guru is perfect, his words ever true;
One might become a saint if he looks at you.

Nanak says:
Countless are his glories, beyond valuation;
With the guru's grace, one can have God's union.

5

Heartfelt thanks to my guru I give,
For helping me become more contemplative.
Beyond all description is the God I behold;
Transcendent and wise, desireless I am told.
Not needing a spoon, fork or chalice,
He gives peace to all and bears none malice.
Many saints offer homage to the One beyond value,
And keep His lotus feet within heart's purview.

Nanak says:
To my true guru I'm a sacrifice;
I repeat God's name through his grace and advice.

6

Obtaining the love of God's name is most rare;
Immortal are those who drink this nectar.
Within whose heart the Lord appears,
That one lives more than a million years.
He always speaks the Lord's holy name,
And the truth about God to his students proclaims.
Unaffected by worldly lures,
Of the Lord alone he's a connoisseur.

Nanak says:
When the lamp of God's name lights up your mind,
Doubt, false love and pain are left behind.

7

A guru brings cool air in the midst of heat;
True joy comes, sorrow is in retreat.
Death and life no longer hold fear,
As the guru's teaching our minds will clear.
Now all fears from wherever do cease;
Devotees from all troubles will be released.
The guru has blessed us with mercy immense;
We repeat God's name in saint's audience.

Nanak says:
Listening to songs in praise of the Lord,
Wanderings are over, our spirits restored.

8

God is the Relative and the Absolute,
Both with and without attribute.
His power continues to fascinate;
His dramas He performs and evaluates.
God is the only Reality to exist;
He pervades all things, from complex to simplest.
He's interwoven in form and color;
At the guru's touch, God's glimpses occur.

Nanak says:
Creation contains His power so great.
To sacrifice to Him is my fate.

CANTO XIX

Prologue

God's worship is all that accompanies our soul;
All worldly things to ashes go.

Nanak says:
The only real wealth is that of His name,
Whose worship and remembrance should be our aim.

1

Consult the holy about God's name;
Dwell on the name, and it proclaim.
O friend, leave off your other effort;
Maintain His words as thy heart's sole escort.
God alone has power to act;
Acquiring His name is the only right track.
Gather this wealth and become truly blest;
To this the saints do clearly attest.

Nanak says:
Endow your faith with this remedy;
Suffering will end, I guarantee.

2

That wealth you seek in all byways
Would be yours by devoting to the guru your days.
The comforts which you ever crave
Come by loving in the saints' conclave.
The glory from doing good deeds would be yours,
If you would submit to the holy Counselor.
Those sufferings that drugs don't treat,
God's name will definitely defeat.

Nanak says:
The treasure of treasures is the name of the Lord!
Remember His name and to heaven you'll soar.

3

If God's name in the mind you cultivate,
Peace will come as mind's wanderings abate.
A man will have no misery or harm,
If God resides in his heart as a charm.
The age is burning, only the name can cool;
Cherishing the name, peace will come; no more be a fool.
Bliss and devotion elevate the mind;
Fear disappears, to hope you're inclined.

Nanak says:
From death's shackles you'll be set free,
And achieve the state of immortality.

4

A true man speaks God's name and becomes immortal;
False ones enter transmigration's portal.
Serving the Lord, wandering will cease;
Go with the guru and leave ego's caprice.
Thus the true goal of life is obtained;
Remember Him Who your soul does maintain.
There is no other way out of this pain;
Vedas, Shastras and *Smritis* are in vain.

Nanak says:
Devote yourself to God Almighty,
And get your heart's desire, rightly.

5

Your wealth cannot be taken along;
Why is your attachment to it so strong?
Of friends, family, sons and wife,
Who goes with you at the end of life?
Entangled in power and worldly joy,
Who can then get freedom unalloyed?
Chariots and harnesses, elephants and horses
Are false displays, worthless and coarse.

Nanak says:
The Giver of these things is hidden from a fool;
He'll repent, he's forgotten the name that's a jewel.

6

O foolish man, heed the Guru's advice:
Intellect without love will never suffice!
Loving the Lord with all your heart
Will to your mind purity impart.
Let the lotus-feet of His words be with you;
To the sins of past lives you'll bid adieu.
Repeat His name, then disperse it wide;
One is saved who keeps the name as his guide.

Nanak says:
The name of God is the essential verity;
Sing His praises with heartfelt clarity.

7

Chanting God's praise is mind's best cleanser;
Pride will no more its perceptions censor.
Remembering the Lord with every breath,
You'll be free from anxiety until your death.
Renounce all mundane calculations;
Seek true wealth in saints' associations.
With His name as your capital continue to trade:
Peace comes now and glory when this world fades.

Nanak says:
Only those favored by fortune can see
The One that's in all, most blessed Thee.

8

Remember the one God, adore Him alone;
Him alone love and desire to be shown.
To the One without bound, praise you should sing;
Repeat His name with all your being.
God is the Absolute, only One,
Our all-pervasive beloved companion,
Who spins out from Himself extensive creations.
Worshipping Him, sins suffer negation.

Nanak says:
Know God is One with the guru's assist;
Heart and soul will be flooded with bliss.

CANTO XX

Prologue

Nanak says:
For so long I have strayed down many blind alleys;
I now wish refuge in Your peaceful valleys.
O Lord, I ask Thee kindly to grant:
That I may serve Thee, ever I am extant.

1

O God, please give Your name to me;
I'm only a beggar, and need your mercy.
I also request the dust of saints' feet;
'Twould fulfill my desires and make me complete.
May I sing praises of Your excellence,
And think of You when breath shall commence.
May my heart yearn for Thy lotus feet;
Serving You would make my days sweet.

Nanak says:
The Lord is my shelter, my sole support;
I want Thy good name to be my consort.

2

Much peace will come if God glances at you;
Those relishing His name are very few.
Who tastes God's name is indeed blessed,
And becomes perfect, never depressed.
They are filled with the wine of love whose flavor
Develops when you're with men drunk on the Savior.
Asking His protection, forsaking any other,
Their minds are illumined, attention on the Father.

Nanak says:
Repeating God's name are a fortunate few;
Attaining real peace are those who do.

3

Obtaining instructions from a true guru,
The servant's desires are fulfilled and are through.
To His servant the Lord is ever so kind;
That makes lasting happiness possible to find.
Slavery does end, freedom will arrive;
Pains of births and deaths will no more revive.
All dreams and longings are now realized;
The servant's with God always, life now idealized.

Nanak says:
He's merged with God to Whom he belongs;
Through love his absorption in the name is most strong.

4

How forget Him, Who rewards all our work;
Whose awareness of our efforts will never shirk?
How forget Him, Who provides everything;
Who is the life of we the living?
How forget Him, our prenatal guide?
The rare man knows this, who's been at the guru's side.
How forget Him, Who saves us from sin,
Reuniting us finally with our Origin?

Nanak says:
These points the guru helps us apprehend;
We must to God always attend.

5

Good friends, make it your business to preclude
All else; on God's name alone do brood.
Remembering the name will bring you peace;
Teach others His name; your practice mustn't cease.
In love and devotion your life is well-spent;
Life ends in ashes if love be absent.
With love of the name good fortune and peace come;
The name helps man swim life's ocean and not succumb.

Nanak says:
For all ills the name is the certain cure;
By remembering it, much goodness you'll ensure.

6

Who loves the Lord and yearns for His name,
Knows that soul and body have worked for this aim.
Seeing God's lover is reassuring;
Washing his feet, my joy is maturing.
Love saturates the beings of such men;
One rarely finds himself in their den.
I have one request to make as a favor:
By the grace of the guru, God's name may I savor.

Nanak says:
The splendor of God I cannot express;
In all that exists the Lord manifests.

7

Kind to the poor, God is forgiving;
Delighted by love, merciful to the living.
God is the world's Protector and Sustainer;
Helper of the helpless, of all the Maintainer.
He's the Original Being, the Cause of everything;
The breath of life if to Him you cling.
Who cultivates divine love and devotion,
And repeats God's name, is freed from false notions.

Nanak says:
We are without virtue, ignorant and low;
O Lord Supreme, protect us from woe!

8

It's heavenly joy, a deliverance to sing
Even for a moment the praises of the King.
Listening to chanting of the name is a pleasure;
Those sounds are regal, great in every measure.
Hearing one's tongue sound the name is akin
To music, good food or fine clothes on the skin.
Who keeps the guru's word in his heart,
That name wealth and virtue to him imparts.

Nanak says:
Who the Lord shall bless and grant dwelling with sages,
Gets comfort and blessings throughout the ages.

CANTO XXI

Prologue

Nanak says:
The Formless is Absolute and differentiated;
In the primordial trance all He contemplated.
Taking up His energy to fashion creation,
The Omnipresent remembers Himself in meditation.

1

When the world had not yet come into view,
Who was there to evil or good do?
When God was in His profound trance,
Strife or hatred had not a chance.
Before there existed color or form,
No joy or sorrow described the norm.
When holy God was the only Thing,
Superstition and attachment to no one could cling.

Nanak says:
The Lord Himself has created this play;
There is no other Author, to Him we should pray.

2

Long ago when there was only He,
What then could be bound or free?
When there was one God, unreachable and limitless,
Who would to heaven or hell have ingress?
When Absolute was in repose,
Where were matter, mind or souls?
Before the Lord dispersed His light,
Who was fearless, who in fright?

Nanak says:
He's the Performer of plays He has writ;
To God there's no access, He's infinite.

3

When eternal God was seated on His throne,
Weren't birth and death completely unknown?
When the Perfect Creator alone existed,
Who feared death, or of what it consisted?
When all was impersonal, ineffable God,
To whom could the karmic accountant nod?
When unfathomed God, beyond matter and mind, was all,
Who was then free, or to whom did fetters befall?

Nanak says:
Unequalled God is full of wonder;
From Himself He created every contour.

4

When immaculate God was still introvert,
What was to be washed, there being no dirt?
When there was only the Formless One, absolute,
Where then were pride or disrepute?
When holy God was all that existed,
Were deception or lies done by the twisted?
When within Himself God's light was contained,
Who could feel hunger or be sated with grain?

Nanak says:
The Creator motivates all that we do;
He extends well beyond our human view.

5

When God still held all glory within,
No one could share it, neither friends nor kin.
When knowledge and wisdom were God's and still latent,
Then where were scriptures or readers to comment?
When His attributes were still withheld,
Where had the good or the bad ever dwelled?
When there was none but God to be high or base,
How could master or slave ever show face?

Nanak says:
We're astonished to see what the Lord has made;
God alone knows how far He does pervade.

6

When there was but He, incomprehensible and veiled,
Who was there to be influenced by goods for sale?
When God bowed to Himself as there was none other,
Who would by the world's attractions be smothered?
When the Absolute One existed alone,
Who would be anxious or feel cares had flown?
When the Lord was within Himself and content,
Who would for talking or listening have a bent?

Nanak says:
Limitless and most exalted is the Lord;
Unequalled by any is the One I've adored.

7

When God gave finite realm extension,
And spread in it three qualities of expression,
There began talk of good and evil.
Some longed for heaven; some found hell their domicile.
Duality, mundane love, ego and fear arose;
Attachments and suffering of the world were imposed.
Now there was pain and comfort too;
Honor and disgrace and gossip grew.

Nanak says:
God is the viewer and performer of this play;
He's alone after drawing within Him these light rays.

8

God is not visible though manifest in the saint,
For whose glory the whole universe God does paint.
He is dispenser of the hidden and seen;
Saints' glory and God's is a private theme.
God has amusements and frolics about,
Enjoying His pleasures yet detached, no doubt.
He chooses some to remember the name,
Causing others to play the worldly game.

Nanak says:
O Lord beyond measure, unfathomed and profound!
At Your behest does this servant expound.

CANTO XXII

Prologue

Nanak says:
The Lord of man and every being
Works in all as their mainspring.

The Lord Himself is all-pervading;
Anyone else would be God masquerading.

1

Transcendent and immanent is the Lord,
Listening and speaking through the human word.
Creating the world when He pleases;
Absorbing in Himself the world, it ceases.
Without God there is nothing, all is still;
He maintains the world by the thread of His will.
To whom God gives this understanding,
Acquires the gift of the name everlasting.

Nanak says:
Whosoever looks on every man equally,
Masters the universe and knows the Reality.

2

All creatures on the Lord depend;
Gracious to the poor and those who cannot fend.
None can destroy who God would preserve;
Nearly dead is the one who from God does swerve.
Leaving Him, for shelter where would you go?
Undeluded, the Lord lives on the highest plateau.
Power over lives is in God's hands,
Who accompanies you throughout all lands.

Nanak says:
God is the Treasure with no limit or end;
This servant his life to God does commend.

3

The Lord of mercy is everywhere present;
Kindness and mercy to all He has sent.
The Knower of each heart pervades all space,
Governing His affairs in every case.
God provides for His creatures in various ways;
They look up to Him, hoping for praise.
Those who God chooses, with the Lord unite;
The chosen worship and laud Him to great height.

Nanak says:
He who firmly believes in the Lord,
Realizes the one God evermore.

4

Remembering God's name, one can be assured
That whatever he hopes for will be procured.
It's service alone that you must engender;
Divine status will come if to God you surrender.
Who keeps the Lord close to his heart,
Never from that highest thought of the name will part.
Day and night he's the guru's devotee,
As worldly bonds break and rancor does flee.

Nanak says:
In this world comes peace, and bliss in the next;
God unites with a servant, ending his treks.

5

In holy company attain bliss divine;
Sing glory to God, the Primal Shrine.
Meditate on the name and its great joy;
Use the body for the path, not a trivial toy.
Chant the immortal words of His praise,
Thus saving your soul from rebirth's days.
Ignorance and darkness will be dispelled;
God's presence for you will never be quelled.

Nanak says:
Let the words of the sages lodge in your heart;
Life's dreams will then have real counterparts.

6

Glorify this life and what comes later,
By always remembering the name of the Creator.
Perfect are the words of the faultless guru;
Realize the truth using his words as a cue.
Call to His name with all you have;
For fear, pain, and sorrow the name is a salve.
O trader, purchase the name and its truth;
You'll have valued wares for the next world's booth.

Nanak says:
Take the Lord alone as your life's support;
Wanderings will end, at your final home's court.

7

Separating from God, where can one go?
Follow the Preserver, Who salvation can bestow.
Contemplate the Fearless One and fears you'll lose;
By His grace you'll be free and with God will fuse.
No pain can afflict who God protects;
Repeating the name, great joy mind collects.
Anxiety dissolves and pride disappears;
None can equal devotee without peers.

Nanak says:
His interests are watched by the brave guru;
Also skillfully done are all he must do.

8

The guru has wisdom, a divine glance;
Mankind is saved by the sight of him, perchance.
The guru's lotus feet are above all treasures;
Divine and charming are his measures.
Honored are those who do him serve;
He's omniscient, a genius, a man of great verve.
Who keeps such a one in his heart is blest:
Death cannot come as it must for the rest.

Nanak says:
Those who meditate on God with the guru,
Attain immortality as their due.

CANTO XXIII

Prologue

Nanak says:
Whose eyes the guru anoints with knowledge
Finds ignorance gone, a supreme privilege.
Who meets a true saint, by God's holy grace,
Receives divine light which his mind will embrace.

1

By the grace of the guru, one finds God within.
So sweet tastes the name the disciple will win.
From God comes the visible world of matter,
So varied in color and form is the latter.
The incomparable name is the source of all joy,
And dwells within every girl and boy.
Spontaneously flows the divine melody;
Beyond description is that wondrous ecstasy.

Nanak says:
Who God blesses with vision enjoys this bliss;
For others it's only a hypothesis.

2

The Lord is infinite, Him you cannot divide;
He exists in the body and also outside.
God is in the earth, the heavens and below,
Sustaining life wherever you go.
He's in the mountains, grass and forests;
All creatures act as He suggests.
God is in water, wind and fire;
Everything contains the One we admire.

Nanak says:
The Lord inhabits every place;
Divine peace will come by the guru's grace.

3

God is in the stars and spaces obscure;
He manifests in flights of thought called scripture.
The language of God is what we speak;
He's poised and steady, never wavering or weak.
Through His power are projected dramas on earth;
Not for purchase are His qualities, priceless is their worth.
God supports the whole, like texture in fabric;
All lights derive from the Lord's candlestick.

Nanak says:
Who through the guru with illusion dispenses
Finds firm faith in God's omnipresence.

4

Saints perceive the Lord in all things;
The kernel of all religions in their heart rings.
Saints have ears for divine hymns solely,
And remain absorbed in the One most holy.
Saints that realize the Truth will live
So that only truth comes when they are talkative.
Whatever happens saints accept peacefully,
Understanding that God decides what shall be.

Nanak says:
God lives outside and within all;
Whoever sees this becomes quite enthralled.

5

God is Truth, as is creation,
Since from Him it gets formation.
When God wishes, expansions He undertakes;
And at His wish, all into One He makes.
God's powers are many, He's beyond our ken;
He has communion with whoever He's chosen.
Who can be near or far from the One?
Present everywhere, no place does He shun.

Nanak says:
God's all-pervasiveness only is seen
When He's shown Himself in your inner being.

6

It is God Who functions in the parts of the living,
And peers from the eyes of each human being.
The whole of creation is the Divine body;
He speaks His praises, enjoying what's auditory.
Having built this stage where will play life and death,
God made illusion to fool most who draw breath.
Residing everywhere, He yet remains aloof,
Behind your speech whether praise or reproof.

Nanak says:
What appears or decays does so by God's will;
Retracting all things by His wish — there is nil.

7

Whatever the Lord decrees is not bad;
To God's world who else is able to add?
The Lord is good, and good what He does;
The Lord alone knows His purposes.
The creation He sustains is true, as is He,
Woven in the texture of all things, yet still free.
His limits and condition must remain unknown,
Unless One like Him can somehow be grown.

Nanak says:
Whatever God does, one must accept;
With the guru's help we'll understand this concept.

8

Whoever finds God shall have comfort and peace;
God unites with him and there'll not be decrease.
In whose heart God dwells come wealth, true honor,
Good family, and salvation to the proprietor.
Thrice blessed is the coming of a man such as this,
Who'll rescue the world from the edge of an abyss.
Inspiring you with vibrations of God's name
Is the purpose of this man, and his sole life's aim.

Nanak says:
Saving himself, others he saves too;
Always bow to this man, he's a true guru.

CANTO XXIV

Prologue

He who remembers the perfect Lord,
Whose name is perfect and so adored,

Nanak says:
With the Perfect One he will be united;
May the praises of God be ever recited.

1

Listen to the teachings that the perfect guru gives;
See the Lord Supreme Who at your side lives.
Remember the Lord with each breath that you take,
And remove the worries which cause your mind to ache.
Cling not to the waves that desire sends along;
In the footdust of saints let your being grow strong.
Relinquish the ego and to God alone pray;
'Cross the ocean of fire, you'll find your way.
In the company of saints this feat can be achieved;
Then the wealth of God's name will at last be received.

Nanak says:
With this divine wealth let your soul be filled,
And bow to the guru, for all this he has willed.

2

Happiness, comfort and serenity of peace
Are enjoyed by the one who has gained his release
From the lure of illusion and foolish pride,
And learned from the guru how to worship God inside.
Drink of the nectar that God's praises afford,
And from hell free your soul through worship of the
　　Lord.
Know in your heart there is one God alone
Who through many manifestations has shown.
The Holder and Sustainer of the universe is He,
As well as the Destroyer of all men's misery.
It is He Who shows mercy for the needy and the poor,
And has compassion for those who others ignore.

Nanak says:
Let His name in your heart never cease to be heard,
For the soul is sustained by this one holy word.

3

The words of the guru are great hymns to be heard;
Priceless gems they are, which to men are conferred.
The man who listens to the message they give,
And according to their guidance is determined to live,
Shall successfully swim across maya's vast ocean,
Saving many others in the wake of his motion.
He is blessed by the Lord (his companions are too)
When God's love permeates his mind through and
    through.
Deep in his heart a divine music plays,
Proclaiming his great victory o'er maya's cunning ways.
These songs of the word bring great joy to his heart,
And with praise to God he responds with his part.

Nanak says:
From the brow of this saint God radiates His light;
Students too can be saved by this being so bright.

4

Hearing that God offers refuge to mankind,
We have come to seek shelter and gain peace of mind.
With the Lord we have now been joyfully united;
Because of His grace, our way has been lighted.
Our hatred has vanished within His embrace;
In the footdust of all we've acknowledged our place.
Remembering the name has caused this transformation,
Which occurred with the help of the guru's mediation.
As servants we've received approval and recognition,
And the grace of the guru brings our work to fruition.
From sin and attachment we have been freed,
For the sound of God's name is all that we need.

Nanak says:
Our cargo has arrived in heaven unimpeded;
Through God's grace, our efforts have at last succeeded!

5

To the Lord give praise my saintly friend,
And with one-pointed concentration let your mind
    attend.
This song of joy has a noble aim:
To speak about God and the praise of His name.
When this song finds a place in some heart that's true,
The owner will embody divine virtue.
For all desires the Lord will provide;
His genius is recognized far and wide;
The highest of heights he will achieve:
From transmigration he'll no more grieve.

Nanak says:
A man leaves the world with the name's well-earned
    treasure,
When the song of joy he's attained in good measure.

6

Eternal happiness, comfort, peace and wealth,
Knowledge, wisdom, spiritual power and health;
Learning, devotion, service and meditation,
Union with God and internal purification;
All blessings of life, immunity from temptation
In the midst of attractions to life's vast creation;
Even the perfect enlightenment of the soul!
Beauty, divine wisdom and knowledge of the whole;
The power to see mankind's equality,
And the realization of oneness in diversity:

Nanak says:
All of these blessings are received by he
Who recites the *Sukhamani* reverently;
And in his concentrated mind is heard
The sound of the guru's most divine name-word.

7

The name is a treasure for whomever it engages;
That person shall be saved in all of the ages.
The praise of God and His name that men bless
Are the subjects that all of the Scriptures address.
In the hearts of God's saints the name does reside;
According to its truth all religions abide.
In the company of the guru all sins are erased,
And by death a man will no longer be chased.

Nanak says:
Only those who the Lord Himself has designated,
Whose destiny on their heads is clearly indicated,
Shall seek the guru who can give protection
And guide them along the path of perfection.

8

Who listens in his heart to God's name with devotion
Always remembers the Lord, that vast Ocean,
Remover of the pains from transmigration:
One's life has reached its consummation.
His mind now hears naught but God's holy name;
His words are like nectar and faultless is his fame.
Duality, disease and sorrow become faint;
All deeds are virtuous, he's now a saint.

Nanak says:
Most glorious and exalted His life shall be,
And thus the divine name is called *Sukhamani*.

About Swami Rama

Yogi, scientist, philosopher, humanitarian, and mystic poet, Swami Rama is the founder and spiritual head of the Himalayan International Institute of Yoga Science and Philosophy, with its headquarters in Honesdale, Pennsylvania, and therapy and educational centers throughout the world. He was born in a Himalayan valley of Uttar Pradesh, India, in 1925 and was initiated and anointed in early childhood by a great sage of the Himalayas. He studied with many adepts, and then traveled to Tibet to study with his grandmaster. From 1949 to 1952 he held the prestige and dignity of Shankaracharya (spiritual leader) in Karvirpitham in the South of India. He then returned to the Himalayas to intensify his meditative practices in the cave monasteries and to establish an ashram in Rishikesh.

Later he continued his investigation of Western psychology and philosophy at several European universities, and he taught in Japan before coming to the United States in 1969. The following year he served as a consultant to the Voluntary Controls Project of the Research Department of the Menninger Foundation. There he demonstrated, under laboratory conditions, precise control over his autonomic nervous system and brain. The findings of that research increased the scientific community's understanding of the human ability to control autonomic functioning and to attain previously unrecognized levels of consciousness.

Shortly thereafter, Swami Rama founded the Himalayan Institute as a means to synthesize the ancient teachings of the East with the modern approaches of the West. He has played a major role in bringing the insights of yoga psychology and philosophy to the attention of the physicians and psychologists of the West. He continues to teach students around the world while intensifying his writing and meditative practices. He is the author of many books and currently spends most of his time in the mountains of Northern India and in Pennsylvania, U.S.A.

The main building of the national headquarters, Honesdale, Pa.

The Himalayan Institute

The Himalayan International Institute of Yoga Science and Philosophy of the U.S.A. is a nonprofit organization devoted to the scientific and spiritual progress of modern humanity. Founded in 1971 by Sri Swami Rama, the Institute combines Western and Eastern teachings and techniques to develop educational, therapeutic, and research programs for serving people in today's world. The goals of the Institute are to teach meditational techniques for the growth of individuals and their society, to make known the harmonious view of world religions and philosophies, and to undertake scientific research for the benefit of humankind.

This challenging task is met by people of all ages, all walks of life, and all faiths who attend and participate in the Institute courses and seminars. These programs, which are given on a continuing basis, are designed in order that one may discover for oneself how to live more creatively. In the words of Swami Rama, "By being aware of one's own potential and abilities, one can become a perfect citizen, help the nation, and serve humanity."

The Institute has branch centers and affiliates throughout the United States. The 422-acre campus of the national headquarters, located in the Pocono Mountains of northeastern Pennsylvania, serves as the coordination center for all the Institute activities, which include a wide variety of innovative programs in education, research, and therapy, combining Eastern and Western approaches to self-awareness and self-directed change.

SEMINARS, LECTURES, WORKSHOPS, and CLASSES are available throughout the year, providing intensive training and experience in such topics as Superconscious Meditation, hatha yoga, philosophy, psychology, and various aspects of personal growth and holistic health. The *Himalayan Institute Quarterly Guide to Classes and Other Offerings* is sent free of charge to everyone on the Institute's mailing list.

The RESIDENTIAL and SELF-TRANSFORMATION PROGRAMS provide training in the basic yoga disciplines—diet, ethical behavior, hatha yoga, and meditation. Students are also given guidance in a philosophy of living in a community environment.

The PROGRAM IN EASTERN STUDIES AND COMPARATIVE PSYCHOLOGY offers a unique and systematic synthesis of Western empirical sources and Eastern introspective science. Masters and Doctoral-level studies may be pursued through cross-registration with several accredited colleges and universities.

The five-day STRESS MANAGEMENT/PHYSICAL FITNESS PROGRAM offers practical and individualized training that can be used to control the stress response. This includes biofeedback, relaxation skills, exercise, diet, breathing techniques, and meditation.

A yearly INTERNATIONAL CONGRESS, sponsored by the Institute, is devoted to the scientific and spiritual progress of modern humanity. Through lectures, workshops, seminars, and practical demonstrations, it provides a forum for professionals and lay people to share their knowledge and research.

The ELEANOR N. DANA RESEARCH LABORATORY is the psychophysiological laboratory of the Institute, specializing in research on breathing, meditation, holistic therapies, and stress and relaxed states. The laboratory is fully equipped for exercise stress testing and psychophysiological measurements, including brain waves, patterns of respiration, heart rate changes, and muscle tension. The staff investigates Eastern teachings through studies

Himalayan Institute Publications

A Call to Humanity	Swami Rama
Living with the Himalayan Masters	Swami Rama
Lectures on Yoga	Swami Rama
A Practical Guide to Holistic Health	Swami Rama
Choosing a Path	Swami Rama
Inspired Thoughts of Swami Rama	Swami Rama
Freedom from the Bondage of Karma	Swami Rama
Book of Wisdom (Ishopanishad)	Swami Rama
Enlightenment Without God	Swami Rama
Exercise Without Movement	Swami Rama
Japji: Meditation in Sikhism	Swami Rama
Sukhamani Sahib: Fountain of Eternal Joy	Swami Rama
Life Here and Hereafter	Swami Rama
Marriage, Parenthood, and Enlightenment	Swami Rama
Path of Fire and Light, Vol. I	Swami Rama
Path of Fire and Light, Vol. II	Swami Rama
Perennial Psychology of the Bhagavad Gita	Swami Rama
Love Whispers	Swami Rama
Celestial Song/Gobind Geet	Swami Rama
Creative Use of Emotion	Swami Rama, Swami Ajaya
Science of Breath	Swami Rama, Rudolph Ballentine, M.D., Alan Hymes, M.D.
Yoga and Psychotherapy	Swami Rama, Rudolph Ballentine, M.D., Swami Ajaya
Yoga-sutras of Patanjali	Usharbudh Arya, D.Litt.
Superconscious Meditation	Usharbudh Arya, D.Litt.
Mantra and Meditation	Usharbudh Arya, D.Litt.
Philosophy of Hatha Yoga	Usharbudh Arya, D.Litt.
Meditation and the Art of Dying	Usharbudh Arya, D.Litt.
God	Usharbudh Arya, D.Litt.

Psychotherapy East and West: A Unifying Paradigm	Swami Ajaya, Ph.D.
Yoga Psychology	Swami Ajaya, Ph.D.
Psychology East and West	Swami Ajaya, Ph.D. (ed.)
Diet and Nutrition	Rudolph Ballentine, M.D.
Joints and Glands Exercises	Rudolph Ballentine, M.D. (ed.)
Transition to Vegetarianism	Rudolph Ballentine, M.D.
Theory and Practice of Meditation	Rudolph Ballentine, M.D. (ed.)
Freedom from Stress	Phil Nuernberger, Ph.D.
Science Studies Yoga	James Funderburk, Ph.D.
Homeopathic Remedies	Drs. Anderson, Buegel, Chernin
Hatha Yoga Manual I	Samskrti and Veda
Hatha Yoga Manual II	Samskrti and Judith Franks
Seven Systems of Indian Philosophy	Rajmani Tigunait, Ph.D.
Swami Rama of the Himalayas	L. K. Misra, Ph.D. (ed.)
Sikh Gurus	K.S. Duggal
Philosophy and Faith of Sikhism	K.S. Duggal
The Quiet Mind	John Harvey, Ph.D. (ed.)
Himalayan Mountain Cookery	Martha Ballentine
The Yoga Way Cookbook	Himalayan Institute
Meditation in Christianity	Himalayan Institute
Art and Science of Meditation	Himalayan Institute
Inner Paths	Himalayan Institute
Chants from Eternity	Himalayan Institute
Spiritual Diary	Himalayan Institute
Blank Books	Himalayan Institute

Write for a free mail order catalog describing all our publications.